WINDSURFING

A Complete Guide

By ROSS R. OLNEY

With Photos By
CHAN BUSH

WALKER AND COMPANY  New York

Library of Congress Cataloging in Publication Data

Olney, Ross Robert, 1929–
Windsurfing: a complete guide.

Includes index.
Summary: An introduction to the history, equipment, beginning and advanced techniques, and competition rules of windsurfing.
1. Windsurfing—Juvenile literature.
[1. Windsurfing] I. Bush, Chan, ill.
II. Title.
GV811.63.W56046 1982 797.1'72 81-71832
ISBN 0-8027-6449-5 AACR2
ISBN 0-8027-6465-7 (lib. bdg.)

ACKNOWLEDGMENTS

The author and photographer would like to thank the following for their advice and information, and for helping with and posing for photographs for this book:

Eric Nonniat, Windsurfing International; Chan Bush III, windsurfer; June Everett, Windsurfing West; Patricia Kuehl, Peter Martin Associates; Maggie Nealis, Windsurfing International; Gale Notestone, windsurfing instructor; Nester Otazu, Control Products; Linda Posnick, windsurfer; Dan Posson, *Wind Surfer;* Leo Robbins, windsurfing instructor; Herb Susskind, Lifeguard, Zero Beach, CA; John Wagar, windsurfing instructor; Laura Wells, photographer; David M. Yost, Editor/Publisher, *Board and Sail;* and especially Con Colburn of Control Products, who helped with this and other of our books and who has been a service to the surfing, skateboarding and windsurfing community since 1959. Con is one of the innovators and master craftsmen in the design and manufacture of these sporting products, and an unselfish contributor to book projects such as this.

First published in the United States of America in 1982 by the Walker Publishing Company, Inc.

Published simultaneously in Canada by John Wiley & Sons Canada, Limited, Rexdale, Ontario.

ISBN: 0-8027-6449-5 Trade 0-8027-6465-7 Reinf.

Book design by Lena Fong Hor

Library of Congress Catalog Card Number: 81-71832

Printed in the United States of America

10 9 8 7 6 5 4 3 2 1

Contents

CHAPTER

1

A Little History

IT IS DIFFICULT TO SAY who really started windsurfing first. Perhaps it was an ancient Polynesian or an early-day surfer. Whoever it was would not recognize the modern sport, or a modern windsurfing shop.

In such a shop are a variety of boards of different sizes and shapes. Multi-colored sails brighten the store. Skegs and daggerboards, the fins that project from the bottom of windsurf boards, are here and there in a mixture of sizes, shapes and styles. There are different masts and different accessories.

There are harnesses, leashes and backpacks. Windsurfing has grown into an exciting modern sport for all ages, a sport that is sweeping this country as it once swept Europe.

So who started it all? Maybe a surfer who drifted too far from shore began it all. Almost certainly some surfer has used a wet suit shirt held to the wind to return to shore.

In 1965, a story appeared in *Popular Science* magazine about a new water sport. It was called "Sailboarding; Exciting New Water Sport." The story, by S. Newman Darby, began, "A sport so new that fewer than 10 people have mastered it promises to become inexpensive sailing fun for many who love to sail, but don't want to have to live with the expense of a full-size boat. Sailboarding is sailing with a difference."

On the open ocean . . .

When doing fancy stunts . . .

In the surf . . .

On a lake . . .

In a sheltered harbor . . .

Darby exhibited his board and sail at shows and noted that several of his outfits were given as prizes on the TV game show "The Price is Right" in 1965.

Perhaps Darby should have remained in the business, but he didn't. Nor, apparently, did he patent some of his ideas.

Meanwhile, Jim Drake was working on the same concept. Who is Jim Drake? Drake is a nationally known authority on U.S. and foreign military systems. He is the co-designer of the X-15 rocket research airplane, the B-70 bomber and the cruise missile. Drake is a renowned engineer and inventor.

Drake was working on his own windsurfer in Santa Monica, California. He began working with Hoyle Schweitzer, another windsurfing pioneer, and eventually sold out to Schweitzer. Hoyle Schweitzer is now the head of Windsurfing International, the world's largest manufacturer of windsurfing boards and equipment.

Who really invented the idea of surfing with a sail? Who cares? The sport is here, and growing at a tremendous rate.

Although it is growing now, it didn't do so at first. During the early days, Schweitzer's boards were generally sold in Europe. The sport had taken hold there in the early 1970's. It became very popular. Only gradually did it return to the United States.

Even in a crowded swimming area, windsurfing is far beyond anything early surfers could have ever imagined.

These signs, or ones like them, are appearing near more and more bodies of water . . . but there is very little other control over the sport.

Now it is rare to see a body of water without the colorful sails of a group of windsurfers. Windsurfing is not limited to the ocean and that is what accounts for the great interest and growth. You need a board and a sail and a breeze and some water . . . *any* water. Desperate people have been known to windsurf across their backyard swimming pool.

A pond, a river, a lake, an ocean—any body of water—and any slight breeze and you can be on your way.

A standard windsurfing board is similar to a surfboard. It is made of the same materials and, at about 11 to 13 feet, is roughly the same size as some surfboards. But there the similarity ends. The standard windsurf board has a daggerboard near the center and one or more smaller skegs at the rear. It has a place for a mast to be inserted. The mast, which carries the brightly colored, windowed sail, is attached to the board by a universal joint. It is not held in a vertical position by any braces or lines.

That's right, the mast can tip over in any direction. The ride is started, in fact, by pulling the mast and sail up out of the water with an uphaul.

Looping around the mast and sail is a wishbone-shaped boom. The boom is tied to the mast and holds the sail out and tight. The windsurfer controls the direction and speed of the unit by movements of the boom which tilts the mast. More about this in the following chapters.

Windsurfing has grown by leaps and bounds in the United States since 1977. More than 500,000 units have been sold by one company alone and there are more and more companies getting on the bandwagon. Windsurfing has been officially designated an event at the 1984 Summer Olympics in Los Angeles.

The versatility of the craft allows a novice to glide across water with only a few brief instructions. Experts can sail at speeds of nearly 30 miles per hour and jump great waves to heights of more than 30 feet into the air.

The windsurfer is the poor man's yacht.

There is a 35-pound, four-year-old boy who is well-known in the sport. Windsurfing attracts others of all ages and physical conditions. Windsurfing as a sport supports two slick-paper, color-filled magazines. (*Windsurf* and *Board and Sail*) and several other publications. There are over 40 companies building boards and equipment in North America alone.

The bottoms of two boards, a standard windsurf board at the left and a high performance board at the right. Note the big daggerboard on the standard board, the multiple skegs on the performance board.

HEAD
ROACH
LEECH
BATTEN
MAST
SLEEVE
108806
WINDOW
INHAUL
CLEW
HANDLE
UPHAUL
FOOT
BOOM
TACK
DOWNHAUL
MASTFOOT

Transportation is easy.

Recently a Frenchman windsurfed from the United States (Alaska) to Russia across the Bering Sea.

Here are some windsurfing facts:

1. Windsurfing equipment lasts almost indefinitely. There is very little wear and tear, unless you are an ocean windsurfer on large waves.

2. You can store your equipment under your bed or in your garage on an overhead rack, out of the way.

3. It takes about 2½ hours per year to maintain your windsurf equipment.

4. To transport windsurf equipment is a one-person job, either behind a bike or on the roof rack of a car.

5. There are no license requirements, no certifications, no tests, no government control over windsurfing.

6. No launching fees are required, nor launch ramps needed.

The parts of a windsurf board.

And learning is quick and simple.

Windsurfing hurts nothing in nature, and leaves no pollution.

7. Homeowner's insurance policies might cover windsurfing equipment and other insurance is available (see Chapter 6 for more insurance information).

8. One person can rig a windsurfer and be sailing in less than 15 minutes.

9. There are no operating costs (fuel, maintenance, etc.) with windsurfing. All you need is water and wind. The only other energy you use is your own.

10. Windsurfing can be learned in a few brief lessons or it can be self-taught, especially with the help of a book such as this.

11. Windsurfing is excellent exercise. In a high wind you get a real workout. In moderate winds you get a passive exercise session and in a light breeze the sport is very relaxing.

12. Windsurfing hurts nothing in the environment, destroys no part of nature, leaves no pollution.

13. Barring careless activities or hot dogging, windsurfing has been proven to be completely safe for all ages.

CHAPTER

2

Getting Ready

THERE WAS A BRAND new motor home in the repair shop at a Southern California dealership. From the driver's seat on back . . . 30 expensive feet back . . . it was waterlogged. Curtains were hanging limply, interior surfaces were warped and cracked, and upholstery and appliances were sodden.

The motor home had been backed down a launch ramp into ten feet of water.

The driver hadn't meant to back all the way. It was just that he was backing his boat trailer down the slope and everything went wrong.

Like the sinking of a great battleship, the motor home went under.

This happens more often than you might imagine as yachtsmen attempt to launch their boats. A wrong gear . . . a slipping brake . . . a wet ramp . . . and down goes the whole rig.

Or how about going down to sail and taking half a day to rig? Once you get the boat in the water there can be up to an hour or two of hooking this line to that cleat and uphauling and downhauling and outhauling. When you finally get going, you can be worn out from getting ready.

Simplicity is the key to windsurfing.

With a good teacher and a simulator you can be on the water in an hour or so.

You have a long, slim, flat boat, a skeg and a daggerboard, a mast and sail and boom. That's it. You can carry it all yourself. You can walk it from your car or bike to the water's edge.

There are no mechanical pulleys, cleats or levers to interfere with you and your fun on the water. In 15 minutes or so you can be rigged and sailing. And you will feel the water with your feet and the wind with your hands through the board and the boom.

It is all very easy.

Even so, it is best to get instruction from an experienced windsurfer, preferably a teacher of windsurfing. Today there are windsurfers wherever there is water. There are windsurfing schools at many of these places.

Most lake vacation areas have schools for windsurfing instruction. Stores that sell windsurfing equipment can guide you to the best instruction. Rivers are regularly windsurfed, so check at the nearest landing. Ocean windsurfing is very popular and schools abound. Check with your local Department of Parks and Recreation for schools.

Leo Robbins is a windsurfing teacher in Ventura, California. He has taught hundreds of students. This, according to most of his students, is the way to go. You can get on the water quicker, according to them, than by learning any other way.

Robbins recalls the young girl from a nearby city who applied for teaching at his instruction course. She knew nothing at all about windsurfing but seemed eager to learn.

After only four lessons she left the school, bought a windsurfing outfit of her own, and quickly became one of the experts on the west coast. Robbins still points to her with pride as one of his outstanding successes.

Many schools have windsurfer simulators that make learning a snap. This is a section of a windsurf board on hydraulic shock absorbers. The board will turn and tilt exactly like a windsurfing board on water. Take the whole unit outside, add a mast and sail, and you are as close to real windsurfing as you can get. Yet an instructor can stand alongside and guide your every move.

With a good teacher and a simulator you can learn and be windsurfing on the water in an hour or so.

You can also learn from a book such as this. You might get a bit wetter a bit more often, but by following the simple guidelines in this book you will learn much faster than by trial-and-error (though

First the instructor indicates the pull of the boom when the wind is blowing.

Then the instructor shows exactly how to stand with back to the wind, sail luffing downwind and board at a right angle to the wind.

you can even learn this sport that way, too).

In any case, doing-it-yourself will not hurt you if you later decide to go to a school.

WEATHER

The best possible place to learn is on a flat, shallow body of water. Shallow means water you can stand in, something about waist-deep. Confine yourself to no more than a couple of hundred yards just in case you have to walk back from the first few sails. You

He did it; now you do it.

might learn to run before the wind quicker than you learn to sail crosswind. Or you might just get blown with the wind. That's why most teachers look for an onshore or downshore wind and try to avoid offshore winds.

If possible, begin on a day when the wind is light, but steady, with no gusts or puffs. If you stay away from tall buildings, tree rows, hills and other obstructions, the wind will be steadier.

The problem with gusts is that winds will bounce the sail around. After an hour or two of practice, you can handle this, but at the very beginning a tricky wind is the last thing you want.

A smaller body of water, a sheltered cove, or a slow running river will be less likely to have currents you must fight. You'll also be able to stay near the shore. Some schools even tether the windsurf board to a pole on shore so that it can't go too far out.

If you do get too far out, drop the mast and sail into the water and kneel down on the board. Haul the mast aboard, bunch in the sail, and paddle your way back in.

EQUIPMENT

Most experienced windsurfers wear some type of wet suit and, if the board is slippery or the bottom dirty, some rubber deck shoes. There are special shoes made for windsurfing if you want to get fancy. The wet suit should be worn even if the water seems warm enough. It is easy to get out there and get so involved that you lose track of time. "Hypothermia" or lowered deep-body temperature can result in water as warm as 68° F, and wet suits are not uncomfortable. It doesn't sound as though they would work, but all they do is hold a thin film of water between the suit and the skin. This water warms and acts to keep the body warm as the rubber of the suit insulates from the outside colder water. If hypothermia, or "exposure" should strike, you can become unconscious, or worse.

Eventually, as you begin to sail away from shore, you will want to get a leash to fasten the mast and rig to the board and you might want to get a harness to fasten yourself to the boom. But on the beach or in a shallow pond (and you might not even get into the water at first) don't worry about these things.

STATE OF MIND

Anybody who can walk can windsurf. Youngsters of 4 or 5 years old have learned, and so have grandmothers and grandfathers. Windsurfing is not a "muscle" sport. You can't *force* the board and sail to do what you want them to do. Windsurfing is a sport of finesse and balance and coordination. Windsurfing does not take strength, but it does take brains.

On the other hand, just because you are a good small-craft sailor doesn't mean that windsurfing will be a snap. It is a learned activity, and windsurf boards do not react as small sailboats do. Remember, the mast on a windsurf board is attached to the deck

Now the instructor sheets in.

So you climb aboard and sheet in.

Rigging is easy. First slide the sail cover off the sail.

with a universal joint. It can tilt in any direction, including all the way down into the water. You may give the appearance of having been dismasted, but that is the way things are supposed to be.

This is the mastfoot going into the maststep.

ON LAND

Setting the mast and sail into the board is done the same way on a simulator as on a real board. The bottom of the mast is attached to a universal joint which is attached to the mastfoot. The mastfoot has a round or shovel-shaped extension that inserts into the maststep of the board. It does not attach or fasten permanently to the board.

It is much easier to carry an outfit that breaks down in this manner. Also, the mast can pull out of the board in an emergency on the water rather than the mast or board breaking. That is why windsurfers attach their mast to their board with a tether called a leash. The mast and sail will generally not blow around in the water but a free-floating board can quickly move away. If the two are attached to each other, they will stay together. Then it won't be much of a job to re-stand the mast and sail on your way.

Set the tightness of the sail with the outhaul (a & b).

THE SAIL

The sail has been slipped over the mast, with the mast sliding into the mast sleeve at the front of the sail. Then the sail is pulled down with the downhaul and back with the outhaul to the rear of the sail, called the "clew." The boom is attached to the mast at the proper height, about your own shoulder height, by a line near the handle. Trailing from the boom near the handle is an uphaul line. This line is used to pull the mast and sail up out of the water when you are ready to get underway.

THE SKEG AND THE DAGGERBOARD

The skeg is a small fin under the rear of the board. Some high-performance boards have two or more skegs. The skeg is fastened to the board in some cases so care must be taken to keep it from hitting the beach or underwater rocks.

The shape and placement of the skeg is important, as you will find as you progress in windsurfing. Don't worry about it at first. The manufacturer of the board you are using has done most of the worrying for you. The skeg will be right for that outfit.

The daggerboard is a larger fin near the center of the board. It slides in as a part of the rigging of the board. Once you are in the water, the daggerboard can be shoved down into position or pulled up partially or all the way depending on sailing conditions.

The daggerboard can break, or break the board, if it runs aground, so care must be taken.

LIFE JACKET

The windsurf board is a built-in lifeboat. It will support and carry you and a partner without sinking. That is why the sport of windsurfing has such a fine safety record. It is difficult to get into trouble if you are never without your own lifeboat. If you fall off, the board stops and you just grab on.

Still, life jackets are mandatory in some areas and well-used in all other areas. Check the laws in your area. Meanwhile, if you are not an excellent swimmer, why not wear one? Modern life jackets are lightweight and comfortable, and they can do no harm.

Install the battens.

Tie the mast to the board with a leash. Note that the downhaul on this rig ties the mast to the mastfoot as well as tightening the sail.

LAND PRACTICE

In the next chapter will be instructions on launching and sailing in the water. A quick session on land following the same instructions will help. You can go through all the motions without worrying about the board moving around under you. This is what a simulator does for you. Or you can use your board (without the daggerboard, and protecting or removing the skeg) in the same way.

Put the board near the water's edge then rig the mast and sail. Then do exactly what the instructions say in the next chapter. Pay attention to the wind, to your body position and to other details.

You will get used to the raising of the sail with a hand to hand motion on the uphaul. You'll get proper foot position set in your mind before the board begins to move. And you'll get the feel of "sheeting in" as the wind fills the sail, but without sailing away.

Study the illustrations. You'll see that it doesn't matter whether you are using a simulator or a real board. The time you spend on the beach will help when you are in the water.

And head for the water.

CHAPTER

3

Launching and Sailing

THERE IS A CLASSIC WAY to launch a windsurfer. But first, remember to *carry* the board and sail to the water. Dragging a board and sail can do real damage. A good way to carry the board is with one hand in the maststep slot and the other arm over the board with the hand in the bottom of the daggerboard slot.

Carry the rigged sail over your head with the boom aligned with the wind direction and downwind of your body. You should have one hand on the mast and the other on the boom with the rig overhead. The sail will merely flap in the wind and will be much easier to handle.

With all of this moving, you will also be certain of wind direction. This is something you need to know before you begin to rig.

When you are ready to rig, put the mast and sail in the water. Then put the board in. If you put the board in first, it will drift away in the wind while you are getting the mast ready.

Be sure the board is all the way in the water. Too much pressure on the skeg (you can lower the daggerboard later) can break it.

Set the mastfoot into the maststep. If you are using a tether to attach the mast to the board (and you should), hook it up. If you are a newcomer, the downhaul and outhaul lines should be moderately tight, keeping the sail reasonably tight. After you've sailed a few times, you can adjust the downhaul and outhaul to wind conditions, and to what you want to do with the board that day.

Try to keep the board in waist-deep water so that you won't run around. Some windsurf boards do not have extra reinforcing in the daggerboard area and around the skeg and can be split by grounding. If this happens, water can get into the board under its fiberglass coating and cause this "skin" to bubble up from the board.

RAISING THE SAIL

Most novices and people who are not involved in the sport of windsurfing are surprised at the fact that the sail of a windsurfer can tip all the way into the water. The hollow mast floats and the sail just lies in the water.

But you don't just hop on and pull the sail up with the uphaul line, especially if you are a beginner. Instead, follow these procedures and you might get a ride the first time. You will already have gone through them on land, on a simulator or on your own board. If not, do them on land first, then go into the waist-deep water and try them. Remember, you want a steady, mild breeze if possible.

The secret to windsurfing is the universal joint on the mastfoot, under a rubber cover.

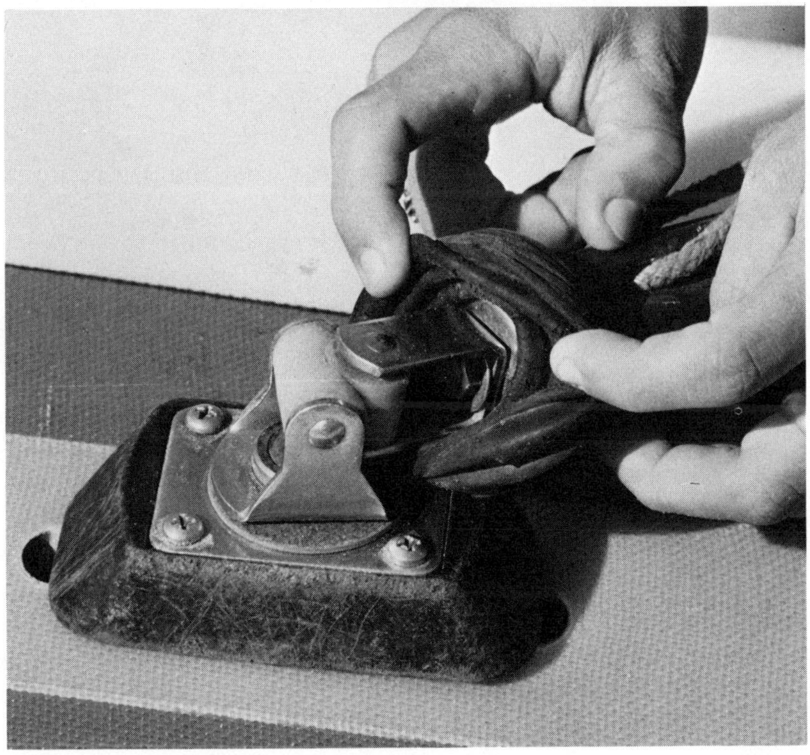

1. Align the board in the water (or on land) so that it is at a right angle to the wind, with the nose pointing in the direction you wish to go and the mast and sail in the water downwind, or leeward. This is *away* from the wind. The mast should be at a right angle to the board.

If the mast and sail happen to be on the upwind side of the board, get it downwind before you do anything else. Lift it just out of the water and swing it over the stern of the board. Step around as you do so until the mast and sail are in the water on the downwind side.

This windsurfer picked a spot before an audience to fall.

2. Climb on the board with your feet on the centerline. The foot nearest the front of the board (the direction you plan to go) should be just forward of the mastfoot. This foot can be touching the mastfoot. The other foot should be directly behind the mastfoot on the centerline.

3. Stand on the board and rock it slightly. Flex your ankles while keeping your hips and knees flexible. Get the feel of the movement of the board on the water. Keep your lower body flexible.

4. Grab the uphaul line, squat slightly and tip your body back. Keep your back straight. Do not bend forward. Gradually raise the

Above. First, align the board in the water so that it is at a right angle to the wind, with the nose pointing in the direction you wish to go, and the mast and sail in the water downwind.

Right top. Foot position is very important. They should be on the centerline and for everything but running, astride the mastfoot. This is on a simulator, here.

Right bottom. When running, or moving about the mast, the feet should still be astride the centerline.

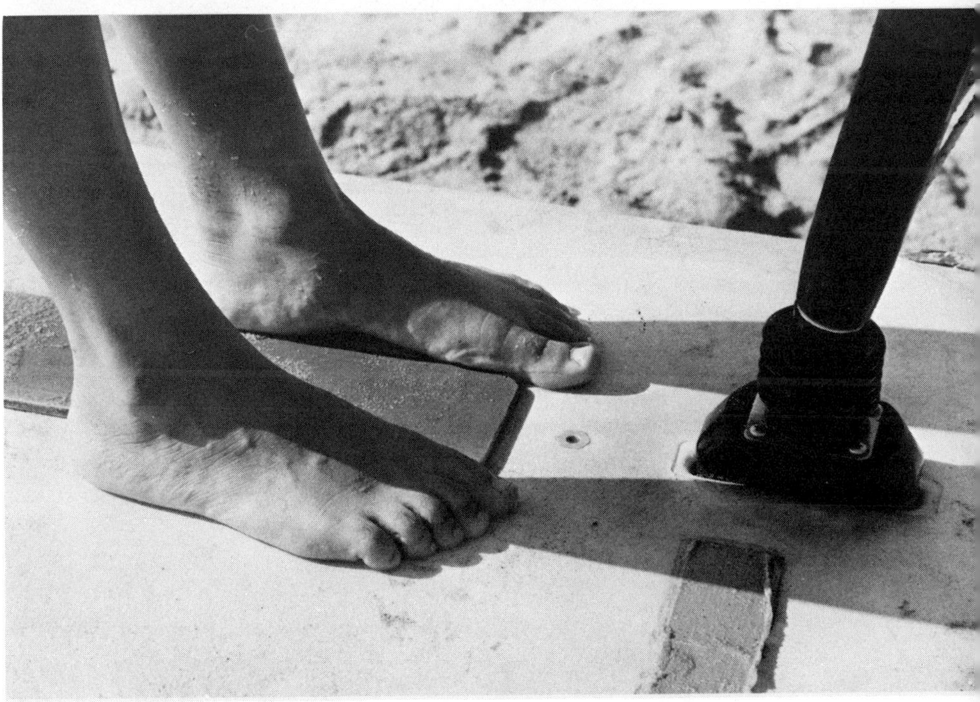

Climb on and put your feet on the centerline on each side of the mastfoot. Grab the uphaul line, squat slightly and keep your back straight. Pull up and allow the water to drain.

sail from the water using your thighs, arms and body weight, not your back. Tuck in your bottom as you lean back to help keep your back straight, and to keep from doing the actual lifting with your back.

NOW WHAT???

The sail is coming up and the wind is acting upon you and the board. Is this all going to work, or not? Don't panic.

1. Relax. The worst that can happen is that you will lose your

Relax. Rapidly pull the mast and sail up.

balance. If that does happen you might be able to prevent a dunking by just dropping the mast back into the water. Otherwise, you will fall in. So what? Start over again.

2. If the sail is coming out of the water, stop for a moment and allow the water to drain. This will lighten it. Keep your hips, knees and ankles loose and your back straight. Keep your feet on the centerline of the board and resist the tendency to tense your legs. Stay loose. You'll soon be doing everything just right by force of habit.

3. Once the water drains, rapidly pull the sail up with the

Raise the mast until the boom end is out of the water and the sail is flapping downwind.

uphaul by hand-over-hand movements until the boom end is completely out of the water. If you leave the boom end in the water the sail may fill with wind and pull you off the board, or at least make you drop the mast back into the water. Make this a quick movement to get the boom up. Try pulling the mast a bit toward the wind so that the wind gives the sail some lift. This will come naturally to you later, but it won't hurt to get the feel right at the start.

4. Hold the uphaul near the boom and allow the sail to flap downwind while you catch your breath for the next move. In this position—feet straddling the mastfoot on the centerline of the board, the sail flapping like a flag in the wind, your back to the wind and the board at right angles to the wind—you can pause. Nothing will happen while you gather yourself.

SOME EXPERIMENTS BEFORE GETTING UNDERWAY

You are still holding the uphaul near the front of the boom. Here's an experiment you can try to give you a better feel for turning the board.

Stretch out your arms so that the far end of the boom is just out of the water, just above the surface. The sail should still be flapping downwind and the wind should be at your back.

Now lean the mast toward the front of the board. Not very far but just a slight lean. You'll see that the bow of the board, the front end, will begin to swing away from the wind. This is called "bearing off" in sailing and windsurfing.

Now lean the mast toward the back of the board, the stern, and the bow will swing back into the wind. This is called "heading up" and is a turn in the opposite direction from bearing off.

Bearing off is turning away from the wind, heading up is turning into the wind.

You don't even have to concern yourself with these specifics just now. The point of this experiment is to show you how the board can be guided one way or the other. When you are underway, you will be steering the board the same way, by tilting the mast fore or aft, to the front or to the rear.

Let's try a tougher test.

As you swing the board into or away from the wind by leaning the mast, take little steps to keep the wind at your back and the sail in front of you. Keep both feet close to the mastfoot. If you begin to lose control, return the mast to the center and the board will stop swinging.

Now for the toughest test of all before you get underway. You are going to turn the board in a full circle by tilting the mast and causing the bow to swing around.

In fact, do it in both directions to continue to improve your control and feel of the windsurfer. During these exercises, fight the tendency to tighten your leg and hip muscles. Keep them as loose and relaxed as possible.

Once you have practiced the following 360° maneuver until you have control, you are ready to get underway. Here is how to turn all the way around, at first into the wind.

Tilt the mast toward the back of the board. The bow will begin to head up into the wind. Take small steps around the mast as the bow continues to swing. Walk around the mast, keeping the sail out in front of you, flapping, and keep the wind at your back.

As the bow swings directly upwind, swing the sail over the stern then tilt the mast toward the bow of the board. This will cause the bow to begin to swing away from the wind, to bear off, to complete one half of the circle. Meanwhile, continue to take small steps around the mast, keeping the wind to your back and the sail out away from you and downwind.

Complete the circle and the board will be back where it started. You will be back on the same side of the board and it will be at a 90° angle to the wind with the sail luffing (fluttering) as it was before.

Now go in the opposite direction by first tilting the mast toward the front of the board. This will cause the board to bear off the wind and you are on the way to a circle in the other direction.

Do these circles until you are in command.

CHAPTER

4

Getting Underway

BY SLIGHTLY LEANING THE MAST forward or aft, you can keep the sail flapping downwind and the board at right angles to the wind.

You might want to get back on land for a little more practice, or you might not need it. What you are going to do is learn how to fill the sail and get underway. On land, you won't have to worry about board balance. You can use either a simulator or you can shove the mastfoot into the sand and try it that way. Try it on the water if you don't mind getting wet. And if you have practiced the circles in the previous chapter you should be ready.

You are standing on the board, feet on either side of the mast and on the centerline of the board. The board is at right angles to the wind, the wind is at your back, and the sail is luffing downwind. You are holding the uphaul near the boom. You are relaxed, with back straight, rear in and legs flexing. In this position, nothing is happening except that you look just *great* out there. You are not moving, though, and everything is under control.

1. Hold the uphaul with your rear hand, the hand nearest the stern of the board. Cross over with your forward hand and take hold of the boom about 10 inches from the mast. At the same time, keep the board at right angles to the wind by tilting the mast forward or to the rear.

2. Here's where things are going to get a little tricky, but be confident. You can do it. It will all be second nature to you once you have learned. Everything will be natural and you won't even have to think about it.

To get underway, hold the uphaul with your rear hand and reach across.

Release the uphaul and with your rear (now your front) hand grasp the boom about shoulder width from your forward hand. (See the illustration.)

3. In one smooth motion, tilt the mast slightly forward past your forward shoulder and slightly to windward, or into the wind. At the same time, pull the back of the boom toward you (this is called

Take hold of the boom about a foot or so from the mast.

"sheeting in") with your rear hand. Turn your body slightly forward in the direction you'll be sailing.

4. If all these motions are done correctly, you'll be moving forward. Keep your back straight and your bottom in. You can tell an amateur from an experienced windsurfer by the way he bends his waist toward the sail. The experts lean away from the sail, using

Then grasp the boom with the other hand and pull in to get underway.

their thighs instead of their waist to control the sail.

5. Keep the mast upright. In stronger winds, tilt it slightly to windward, into the wind. Don't allow the mast to lean away from the wind or you will be pulled over into the water and you'll have to start all over again. It is even possible to get tossed into the water well ahead of the board, so be careful in stronger winds.

6. Once you are underway, bring the mast back away from the bow or you will bear off the wind. Find a foot position that is comfortable. In a stronger wind, lean back to counterbalance the sail. Don't bend forward at the waist, the sign of a beginner.

7. If you feel the sail pulling you over, empty some of the wind from the sail by shoving away with your back hand. Keep the mast close with your front hand. If you are being pulled overboard, let go with your back hand and the sail should luff free in the wind. If worst comes to worst, you can simply let go of everything and the mast and sail will fall into the water.

But pulling up the mast is tiring. One of the reasons why beginners wear out is because they must pull up the sail more often than experienced windsurfers. You might be able to grab the uphaul as the mast starts over, preventing it from going all the way into the water.

Turn slightly in the direction you are going and lean back slightly. Don't bend at the waist—the sign of a beginner. *(International Windsurfer Class Association photo)*

STEERING THE WINDSURFER

By now you know that to change directions you change the lean of the mast. Tilt it toward the bow and you will turn downwind, toward the stern and you will turn upwind. Practice by sailing a zig-zag course, turning one way and then the other.

COMING ABOUT

Sooner or later you are going to run out of water. You can't go on forever. You are going to reach the far shore, or be so far out that you feel you must turn back. You must turn around, or "come about" in sailing terms.

Fortunately, you have already learned the basics of this when you learned to turn the stationary board through 360 degrees. More about turning around in the next section.

Speaking of quick turnarounds, have you ever wondered why the same names appear on the sports pages of newspapers time after time? Are these people lucky, or as good as they seem? Have they really become that expert in their sport?

In most cases, yes. They have become highly skilled at what they do and that is why they win most often. Take Ken Winner, for example, during the 1981 Pan-Am Windsurfing World Cup in Hawaii. Winner was far ahead in the long-distance race. This is a race of more than 18 miles through all kinds of water and weather conditions. Strategy must be carefully worked out well ahead of the event. Board size, sail size and shape, skeg and daggerboard size and configuration, all must be very carefully considered.

Winner had planned very successfully, for the race seemed to be in the bag. The others were well astern of him. But sailing along at a good clip he confidently rounded an island marking the course. Then he realized that he had come around on the starboard side of the island.

The course had been laid out all-marks-to-port.

He had gone on the wrong side of the island.

What does a superior windsurfer like Winner do in such a situation? One thing he doesn't do is give up, or quit. He quickly came about and sailed back around the island so that he would be back on the correct course. By the time he rejoined the field he was in fifth place.

To change the direction of a windsurfer, you lean the mast forward or aft.

You can go in almost any direction you want on a windsurfer. These two, in fact, are going in opposite directions with the same wind.

Sailing at the very peak of his great ability, Winner caught the others one by one and skimmed across the finish line in first place.

SAILING DIRECTIONS

Picking a direction to sail is not quite as easy as if you were walking. When walking or driving, you can go in any direction, even directly into the wind.

Not in sailing. In sailing you can go almost every direction, but not quite. Since you are using wind to move yourself, you cannot go directly into the wind. But you can go into the direction from which the wind is coming. If the wind is coming from the north, and you want to sail north, you can.

It will just take a little longer to get there, since you will be sailing northeast and then northwest, back and forth, until you wind up due north from where you started.

But let's look at the easy-to-understand sailing direction first. Everything in sailing has a special name, and so does this first direction. When you sail *with* the wind, when you go in the same direction as the wind is blowing, you are "running." The sail is out at right angles to the board and you are skimming along.

When you are sailing across the wind, or at a 90° angle to the wind, you are on a "beam reach." Halfway between these two,

Three different directions with the same wind.

between running and a beam reach, is a "broad reach." All of these are with the wind or directly across the wind.

But suppose you want to go *into* the wind, or at least almost into the wind. Visualize a clock face with the wind coming from high noon. If you are sailing toward six o'clock, you are running. Toward four or five o'clock and you are broad reaching. The same is true with seven or eight o'clock. Toward three o'clock or nine o'clock and you are beam reaching.

Any sailboat, and any windsurfer, will also easily sail toward ten o'clock or two o'clock (close reaching) and eleven o'clock and one o'clock (close hauling). A close reach and a close haul are almost directly into the wind, but not quite. Experts say these are easier and much more fun, too.

From directly with the wind to almost against the wind you have, in order: running, broad reaching, beam reaching, close reaching and close hauling.

TACKING

If you want to go directly into the wind, you must "tack." This is a series of zig zag courses going first to one o'clock and then to eleven o'clock. Then back to one o'clock again, back and forth, back and forth. It will take longer to get there, but eventually you will get to that twelve o'clock destination.

Tacking to any destination upwind is called "beating" in sailing terms.

Tacking brings another sailing maneuver, and of course another sailing term, into the picture.

Let's say you have decided to sail to a point across the lake directly into the wind from your position. You will start out from your position by sailing a close haul one way or the other just off the wind, at an angle to where you want to go. After a period of time, and you must judge this, you will change course to close haul on the next leg back across to the other angle. Otherwise, you would sail straight across on a close haul and land far down shore from where you want to be.

Here's what to do to go from one tack to the other.

Lean the mast to the rear. This will bring the bow into the

This sailor could be in some trouble.

152133

wind. Drop the boom but hold the uphaul. The bow will continue to swing. Walk around the front of the mast. The sail will flap over the stern, so help it around. Then place your hands in position on the other side of the sail. Hands on the boom, mast forward, sheet in, and you will sail off on the new course of your zig zag.

After you gain some experience, you will step around the mast with your hands on the mast and boom, not the uphaul line. Either way you will zig and then zag on one tack and then the other and then back to the first until you reach your destination. You will have sailed to a point directly into the wind, a seemingly impossible task.

JIBING, GYBING, OR WHATEVER

Sailing terms have passed down through the ages. Most of them came from the days of sailing ships. They are romantic-sounding terms that even today say exactly what is to be said. Jibing is the same way, except that it has new spellings including gybe, gibe, jibe, or even jib.

They all mean the same. They mean the act of the boom coming across from one side of a sailing craft to the other when running before the wind. If you tack, you are turning into the wind. If you fall off and turn away from the wind, you jibe. When tacking, the bow of the board passes through the "eye" of the wind, the direction from which the wind is coming.

When you jibe, or turn the opposite way, the *stern* of the board passes through the eye of the wind.

If this isn't clear to you, don't worry about it. It'll all make sense when you get out on your board, with the boom in your hands.

To turn downwind with a jibe the sail will swing across the bow of the board as you stand facing forward with your feet on either side of the mast. Here's how.

Tilt the mast forward. This will swing the bow off the wind. The board will bear off. Soon the bow of the board will be straight downwind. The stern of the board will move on through the eye of the wind.

Bring your forward foot back and place it beside your rear foot so you face the bow with a foot on each side of the board. Grab the uphaul and let the sail swing across the bow of the board.

Help the sail on around till it is at right angles to the board. Step on around the mast and sheet in to set the sail and get underway on your new course.

These basic maneuvers will allow you to sail to any point on the compass regardless of the direction of the wind.

LET'S PRACTICE

One of the best ways to practice windsurfing is to sail in small circles, first one way then the other. By sailing in a circle, you will use all of the basic maneuvers listed here and you will soon become skilled at sail-handling and going where you want to go.

Start off on a beam reach then head up to a close reach and finally a close haul. Then tack around quickly by tilting the mast back till the end of the boom touches the water. This will bring you into sailing position on the other side.

Now bear off until you are running, jibe and come back through a broad reach to a beam reach. The circle is completed. Try this exercise around a point, a buoy or a boat or some other fixed spot in the water. By having a fixed point to refer to, your control over the board will be improved.

Next, go the other way—the opposite direction. Once you can sail these circles, you are ready to really begin to enjoy windsurfing.

Experts consider a close reach, very near into the wind, as the easiest to sail. Under this wind direction, the board (or boat, for that matter) responds best to the touch of the experienced sailor.

The toughest to sail? A broad reach, according to experienced sailors, is toughest. What might appear to the novice to be easiest is really the most difficult. Add choppy water to a broad reach and you have the toughest of all for a windsurfer. The board tends to dig its nose into choppy water, an action known as "purling."

FALLING

Windsurfers probably wouldn't get involved in the sport if they didn't like water. Many of them (but certainly not most of them) started as surfers. Everybody who windsurfs enjoys the water. All of this is only to lead up to the fact that if you windsurf, you are going to get wet—if not while learning the basic moves (which is when it will happen over and over) then while perfecting more advanced moves.

Watch the experts sail to get good pointers. Here's one.

In fact, dropping the mast and falling into the water stops your motion completely, and is an acceptable basic move while learning. You are going nowhere and neither is the craft. Falling gives you time to think and get ready for the next try.

You can also be tossed off the board if you try hard enough and do everything wrong. This can occur in a strong wind during a sailing maneuver when the wind suddenly fills the sail before you are ready. Some windsurfers have landed several feet in front of their board.

Keep your weight low to prevent these and other falls. You can sheet out with your rear hand and spill the wind from the sail if you feel trouble coming.

Beginners are often pulled into the sail by the boom due to a sudden gust. Sheet out. If the wind pulls you over into a bend at the

Here's another.

And still another, coming head-on.

waist, squat slightly as you straighten your back and roll your hips downward.

You can let go with your back hand and allow the sail to flap, spilling all the wind, as you squat all the way down. Hold the uphaul with your forward hand to prevent the mast and sail from falling.

It is possible to fall the other way, too. You can fall backwards if a sudden lull in the wind allows the mast to tip over your way. If this happens, squat as before, but this time sheet in the sail with your rear hand to try to use every bit of wind available.

When you are sailing very close to the wind, the wind can shift slightly and knock you down because it gusts in from the other side. A close haul can be tricky on a blustery day. If a gust hits, try to get the mast forward as quickly as possible to prevent heading up, since that's when the wind will most likely slam the other way.

A COUPLE OF TIPS

Windsurfing is becoming more and more popular every day. One of the best ways to learn is to watch somebody with more skill than yourself. Pick out some experts at your windsurfing area and watch how they sail. Then try to match your own style to theirs.

As your skill increases, you'll find that leaning the mast toward the front or rear of the board will work, but that leaning the mast in the direction of the front or rear of the boom will work even better. If you tilt the mast toward the front in the direction the boom is pointing, you'll bear off even more smoothly. If you tilt the mast in the direction the rear of the boom is pointing, you'll head up the same way.

NATURAL HAZARDS

On top of everything else, there are certain natural hazards you must be aware of. You know that you should not run aground or you can break your board, skeg or daggerboard. Weather is something you must always be thinking about. Other boats can leave debris (hatch covers, cargo, etc.) that can quickly wreck a windsurfer. One windsurfer found that he had entangled his foot in a Portuguese Man-O-War, a slithery, mushy sea creature that stings when angered.

Then there was the plight of one champion windsurfer at a major ocean meet. He was racing along well up front until he suddenly came upon a slumbering turtle.

A *big* slumbering turtle.

The board and turtle came together hard. Irritated at being awakened so rudely, the turtle glared at the windsurfer then slowly paddled away to calmer waters.

But the windsurfer was stalled. Both the daggerboard and skeg had been broken off in the collision. The champion was out of the contest.

CHAPTER

5

Buying a Board

IN WINDSURFING, there are three broad types of boards to be considered. Then within these classes are many different types of boards to suit the tastes of different windsurfers. At the end of this chapter will be a list of board manufacturers where you can write for more information.

LEARNING BOARDS

Wide, long, flat, stable boards with less sail area are much more forgiving of mistakes. Some of these boards have a keel for greater stability. Most often, this type of board can be found in the fleet of the local windsurfing school.

You are only going to learn once and this board will be a good one to learn on. It is built for beginners and will minimize your mistakes.

But unless you have a school, or a group of people to teach, this board might not be best for you. It will cost almost as much as a regular recreational board, and yet it will only serve as a learner. It will not perform as you might eventually want it to perform after you have achieved some skill. It won't be as responsive as a regular board. It won't have the sail area, or the quickness on the water.

Perhaps you can afford a board upon which to learn, and another board to use from then on. If you can, go for this board first.

Boards come in a variety of types.

If not, look into the next category, which is still only a middle ground between learners and expensive, specialized boards for free-style, racing and other specific uses.

Although it has been proven that almost everybody can learn to windsurf, you could be the exception. If that is the case—if you simply cannot seem to get the hang of it on a regular board—then this board might make the difference and get you started.

RECREATIONAL BOARDS

The majority of windsurf boards are in the category of recreational boards.

This type of board is not too far advanced for the beginner. But it will still fill the needs of the experienced windsurfer who looks for a challenge.

If you want fun and excitement but are not interested in competing (except for racing with others in this very large class) then this is the board for you. It will offer you speed and excitement after you have learned. Most of the companies listed at the end of this chapter build these boards.

This board has a relatively flat bottom which offers stability. The flat rear of the board gives an ideal planing surface for speed.

Not all recreational boards are totally flat. Some have curved sections, a feature that can help you in upwind performance while costing a little in stability. The flatter the board bottom, the more stable that board will be. A recreational board is built in the same spirit with which a decathlon champion trains. The champion may not be the very best at any single thing, but overall he does everything very well indeed. Overall, a recreational windsurf board is versatile.

Consider the following points when selecting a recreational board. A board should be buoyant enough to support you but if it is too buoyant it will be hard to control in stronger winds. If it is not buoyant enough, it will be unstable.

Stand on the board in the water. If the water comes more than halfway up the side of the board, the board is not buoyant enough for you. If rocking the board front to rear is very difficult, it is too buoyant for you. The average board weighs around 45 pounds.

For all sexes. *(International Windsurfer Class Assn. photo)*

Here are three super-high-performance boards from Control Products. Top (a) and bottom (b).

Most of the boards in the recreational classification are around 12 feet long and about 27 inches wide. But these measurements vary.

A recreational board, ready to sail with all rigging, will cost around $900 to $1200.

RACING AND HIGH-PERFORMANCE BOARDS

Eventually you might want to get into serious competition. Before you rush out to buy a new board, remember that one of the largest racing classes is a recreational board. Certain recreational boards, built for the windsurfer looking for fun, are also raced competitively very often.

Boards built strictly for racing are shaped differently and have much less stability. They may have curved sections at the front for

upwind and light-air performance. The shape will flatten out at the rear so that the board will plane on the surface of the water. Such a board will do well on a triangular sailing course. But it will be difficult to sail for fun because you must always be in instant command, especially if you are sailing downwind.

These boards generally have two or more skegs.

Different racing boards have different characteristics. Some of them are faster in choppy water but slow on smooth water. Most are more difficult to control and not the best choice for leisure sailing.

There is another type of board built especially for surfing and wave-jumping. Wave-jumping is an astounding activity. The sailor sails into a wave and at just the right moment, just before it breaks, sails up the wave and into the air.

Then, up until the last year or so, the windsurfer bailed out. The two, the board and the sailor, dropped back into the water separately with a great splash for each. Today the trick is to stay with the board, to ride it back down. Footstraps are provided on the deck for this purpose.

Experts say that you need only a six-inch chop to wave-jump (if the wind is strong enough). You can imagine what they do on big Hawaiian surf.

The wave-jumping board is really a high-wind board. It is smaller, lighter, narrower and usually has a narrow stern and two or more small skegs at the rear instead of a daggerboard. A daggerboard or a large skeg would be ripped out anyhow. This makes the board difficult, if not impossible, to sail upwind in any kind of a breeze, so it must be considered a specialty board.

MASTFOOT AND MASTSTEP

Every board needs a maststep that will firmly hold the bottom of the mast—the mastfoot—but will allow it to pop out under certain conditions. It is far better, for example, for the mast to pull out of the maststep instead of breaking off under a heavy lateral strain.

Yet, one of the most common complaints among windsurfers is that the mast tends to pull out of the board too easily.

The maststep must hold the mast when it is dry or wet, sandy or clean, brand-new or getting old. Yet under all of these conditions the mast must be removable without strain when you are finished windsurfing for the day.

There are different mastfeet and maststeps from different manufacturers. One of the most common is the blade-type friction method called a "tee" because of its shape. There is a slot in the board and a shovel-shaped blade at the bottom of the mast. Push it into the maststep firmly and it will hold. As it gets older and worn, wrap duct tape around it to make it tight in the step again.

Some boards come with an O-ring system. A rubber O-ring holds the mastfoot into the maststep.

With the adjustable system, the third popular type, a spring-

A recreational board is longer, flatter and easier to handle than high performance boards.

loaded ratchet expands and holds the mastfoot into the maststep. You will decide what you want after reading material from the manufacturers and trying out different systems.

BOOMS

Booms, also called wishbones, are usually made of round, hollow stock. A round boom is easier on your hands and has better strength characteristics. Booms made of oval-shaped material are often used for racing and other high-performance tasks. Such booms will not bend as easily.

A fuller boom, with more of a flare-out from each end and more like racing booms, makes for less sail distortion. But they are not as easy for a novice to master.

The boom should attach to the mast securely. Most booms tie to the mast.

DAGGERBOARDS

Just as different manufacturers offer different boards, maststep combinations, sail windows, booms and other equipment, they also offer different daggerboard sizes and systems.

A standard daggerboard simply slides down through the slot from the top. You can have the daggerboard in the up position as you are getting ready, then shove it down with your foot as you get underway. Or it can be pulled part way up for certain wind conditions. But this daggerboard won't give laterally or fore-and-aft and can break off if you hit something.

If it doesn't break off, it can damage the board if it hits something hard enough.

Kick-up and pivoting daggerboards will snap up out of the way when they hit something, but being more complex they are more prone to problems. The thing you want from a daggerboard is for it to stay down when you want it down and to do no damage if you run aground.

Wave jumping boards are shorter, have multiple skegs and no daggerboard.

TRY BEFORE YOU BUY

Windsurfing shops are not like car agencies. You can't just pick a model and take it out for a weekend of testing before you hand over the cash. Occasionally, but not generally, some shops will allow a test ride. You should test everything, or at least everything you can, depending on the shop's policy.

A test is the best way to determine if a particular board and rig is for you. But not merely a test sail: Carry the board and rig. Rig it and unrig it. Do the things you will do with the board after you become the owner and sailor. Don't allow that wild window design to sway you unless you can really see through it. Bright colors are very pretty, but they won't help you be a better windsurfer.

Take into consideration whether or not you are a brand new sailor, an experienced sailor, or whether you are really looking for a high performance board. Also take into consideration the water and weather conditions you will normally encounter. Your own size and weight must be considered, and even your general fitness and strength.

Watch other windsurfers in your area. Talk to them. Determine the type of boards and rigs they are using. Talking to more experienced people is one of the best ways of all to narrow down your choice of boards.

WINDSURFER MANUFACTURERS

AMF ALCORT SAILBOATS
P.O. Box 1345
Waterbury, CT 06721

ASI
879 W. 16th St.
Newport Beach, CA 92663

AMERICAN SAILBOARD CORP.
7715 Chevy Chase Dr., Suite 101
Austin, TX 78752

CALIFORNIA WINDJAMMER
Box 854
Encinitas, CA 92024

CON SURFBOARDS
CONTROL PRODUCTS
P.O. Box 5685
Santa Monica, CA 90405

CONNELLY SKIS, INC.
20621 52nd West
Lynnwood, WA 98036

CURTIS FUNSURF, INC.
3773 S. Van Dyke
Marlette, MI 48453

DOWNWIND CORP.
1 Pine St.
Nashua, NH 03060

DUFOUR SAILBOARDS
P.O. Box 3558
Stamford, CT 06905

ESKAY PLASTICS, LTD.
2565 Le Corbusier Blvd.
Chomeday, Laval, Quebec
Canada H7S 2E8

FREEBOARD SAILING, INC.
330 7th Ave.
New York, NY 10001

FUNSURF, INC.
300 White St.
Cobourg, Ontario
Canada K9A 4R5

G.S. SPORTS
223 Interstate Road
Addison, IL 60601

HOWMAR BOATS, INC.
29 Mack Drive
Edison, NJ 08817

KRANSCO
501 Forbes Blvd. #118
S. San Francisco, CA 94080

LRF ENTERPRISES, INC.
1126 Sibley St., B
Folsom, CA 95630

M.L. IMPORTS, INC.
Blackburn Center
Gloucester, MA 01930

PERFORMANCE SAILCRAFT
550 Delmar Rd.
Point Claire, Quebec
Canada H9R 4A6

PERFORMANCE
WIND SPORTS
2773 Shelter Island Dr.
San Diego, CA 92109

P & K MARKETING, INC.
1234 Broad St.
Columbus, OH 43205

RAT SPORTS, INC.
1501 Chenier
Les Cedres, Quebec
Canada J0P 1L0

SAILBIRDS
P.O. Box 40-2867
Miami Beach, FL 33140

SAILBOARD INTERNATIONAL
137 Newbury St.
Boston, MA 02116

SAILRIDER, INC.
Box 50, RR 2
South Salem, NY 10590

SAILS ENTERPRISES, INC.
P.O. Box 283
Cummings, GA 30130

SURF-SAILING
INTERNATIONAL
1125 Aerowood Dr.
Mississauga, Ontario
Canada L4W 1Y6

WINDSURFING
INTERNATIONAL, INC.
1955 West 190th St.
Torrance, CA 90509

You'll find that complete outfits will range from a low of about $599 to a high of about $1295. That's for everything, ready to sail. The difference in price comes from a difference in equipment.

Boards will be made of either hand-laid fiberglass, polyethylene or vacuum-formed ABS. Each of these materials cover a polyurethane foam core.

Fiberglass construction gives extra stiffness to the board so it will hold its shape. But it can crack upon impact with something hard. Resulting holes can, however, be repaired without a lot of trouble.

Polyethylene boards won't crack as easily, but they also won't hold their shape quite as well either. Also, they are more difficult to repair if they are damaged.

The middle ground between these two is the ABS board. These are stiffer than polyethylene, but not as brittle as fiberglass.

There is one more board, a simple foam board without an outer shell at all. For fun this board will work. It is easy to handle and doesn't mind if you make a mistake or two. It is also cheaper than the three most popular types. But don't expect high performance from it.

CHAPTER

6

Windsurfing

SAFETY

THIS SECTION WILL BE SHORT and to the point. Then we'll get on to sailing.

Most boats move *through* the water. With good winds, windsurf boards plane on top of it. They skim over the surface at a good clip. You can actually go *faster* than the wind, impossible as that might seem. But don't laugh. Iceboats, with their very low drag characteristics, have been clocked at several times the speed of the wind.

One young windsurfer misjudged his speed and at the same time failed to take into consideration the specific meaning of point number 6 in the following list. At one busy harbor in southern California, a place where hundreds of windsurfers play, there is a narrow channel at the mouth. Through this channel passes the traffic for the harbor.

Big boats, small boats, powerboats and sailboats, and many, many windsurfers, ply this waterway. One large powerboat was heading in just as a windsurfer tried to head across.

The pilot of the motorboat watched as the windsurfer looked back and forth, attempting to judge his speed and position. Could he make it across in front of the powerboat or would he have to bear off and give up the right-of-way?

He decided to go for it.

Sheeting in, he sped across the channel as the motorboat bore down. He almost made it.

But not quite.

Windsurf boards plane on top of the water.

Cleanly over the middle of the board plowed the huge boat. All of the rules of the road about sailboats having the right-of-way were forgotten as the big boat drove the windsurf board under. The mast pulled free and the sail drifted off to one side. Then the board popped up alongside the hull of the motorboat. The sailor, meanwhile, had jumped free and was treading water nearby. He knew he should have waited.

Fortunately, except for a deep nick in the side of the windsurf board, little damage had been done to equipment and none to humans. The windsurfer, in fact, apologized to the captain of the motorboat and then both sailed on.

If you think driving defensively is important, remember also that sailing defensively is important.

The famous saying, "Oh Lord, Thy sea is so large and my boat is so small," holds especially true for windsurfers.

Read through this safety list; then get ready for some fun.

1. Sail near shore until you have gained experience.

2. In lighter winds, use a fuller sail. In stronger winds, pull in on the outhaul and downhaul for a tighter sail.

3. Keep an eye on a reference point on shore so you know exactly where you are.

4. Watch for currents by watching for swirling water or eddying around a buoy. Currents can carry a beginner away.

5. Keep an eye on the weather. It can change quickly. The mast can act as a lightning rod in a thunderstorm, so get ashore promptly.

6. Learn the rules of the road. Even when you have the right-of-way, remember that you are probably the smallest boat in the water.

7. Don't use a harness until you can handle the windsurf board in winds over five knots.

8. Small sails (25 to 30 sq. ft.) can be used for teaching. Medium small sails (40 to 50 sq. ft.) can be used by beginners or in winds over 20 knots by experts. Standard sails (55 to 60 sq. ft.) are good for recreational windsurfing. Larger sails can be used where wind is always lacking.

9. Be sure to use a leash between the board and the mast, especially in stronger winds.

10. Avoid hypothermia (exposure) by wearing a wet suit in colder water. You can lose consciousness in water as warm as 68° if you stay too long.

11. Practice on the beach before going into the water, especially if you are going to try a new maneuver.

12. Avoid sailing downwind of tall obstacles that might cause air turbulence.

13. A towing eye, a ring on the front of the board, is mandatory on boards in Europe and could become so in the rest of the world. Consider installing one on your board.

14. Don't be enticed by fancy windows. Get as large a window as possible for best safety.

15. A daggerboard can, under certain circumstances and speed conditions, try to plane, tipping the board on its edge. Reach down and pull the daggerboard up halfway, or pull it all the way out and hang it on your arm under these conditions.

16. Sheet in as quickly as possible in choppy water. The board is less vulnerable to rocking while underway.

HOTDOGGING

That's exactly what it *is*. What it is called is "freestyle" windsurfing, but what it appears to be is *wild*. As you gain experience, you can give some of these tricks a try. Sure, you'll get wet and you might even get some bruises, but aside from pure sailing these tricks are part of the attraction of windsurfing. These tricks are one of the high points of a windsurfing competition as windsurfers sail back and forth and around judges doing their routines.

This is an area of windsurfing where you can get some real help by watching an expert do a trick before you try it. It will also help if you practice the movements and sail handling on land before you try it on the water. Stick the mastfoot into the sand and work out the routine on the beach. Or remove the daggerboard and protect the skeg and practice on the beach.

Try hard to do the trick correctly. Visualize what you should look like before you begin. Try to have a perfect mental image of what you are doing. In most sports (and in most activities, for that matter) it will help if you will try this "imagery" technique of visualizing the activity ahead of time in your mind.

The more often you make an incorrect move, the more it will be set in your routine. If you are doing something and it is going wrong, stop and try to think about what you are doing. Go back a

Hotdogging, or freestyle windsurfing, is fun . . . once you have gained some experience. *(International Windsurfer Class Assn. photo)*

4243

Wave-jumping will always be one of the truly spectacular tricks on a windsurfer. Will he be able to ride it down?

step and get it right, then go forward again. Don't allow poor windsurfing habits to get too strong a hold on you. Bad habits are hard to overcome.

You have the ability, by now, to rig and launch your board. You have practiced sailing in circles both ways and to a destination. You have learned to master your board under varying conditions.

Here are some freestyle tricks a beginning sailor might try. Some will come easily to you, other will be difficult. They are also difficult for an experienced sailor at first.

As you progress, more tricks will come to mind. There are hundreds of variations being done by experienced sailors in freestyle contests around the world.

Tandem riding is fun and doing tandem tricks is one of the newest things in windsurfing. *(International Windsurfer Class Assn. photo)*

A combination "rail-ride" and "head-dip" is not easy.

HEAD-DIP

With a firm grip on the boom and sailing on a close reach, arch your back and bend your knees as you touch your head to the water. The sail, if you keep it full, will support you as you go all the way over backwards. If the wind should gust, or drop off, you will certainly go in head first.

Back-to-back is a demanding trick for an expert.

BACK-TO-BACK

Tired of hanging onto the boom? Try leaning against the downwind, or leeward, side of the sail, next to the mast. You'll have to sail on a close reach, one of the easiest ways to sail and one that offers the firmest mast and sail. Grasp the mast and step around to the lee side. Turn your back to the mast, sheet in and lean back. Your weight against the back side is the same as your weight hanging on the boom on the front side.

You still may end up being pushed over into the water, so try to feel and judge the wind very carefully.

HELICOPTER

A beautiful trick that involves rotating the sail through a complete circle: Begin by sailing a beam reach, then tilt the sail toward the wind. Allow the sail to flap as you tilt the mast. Rotate the sail so that the back of the boom passes over the bow of the board. Be prepared for the wind to help you complete the full circle of the sail. Sheet in, get into sailing position, and keep going.

DUCK-TACK

Head up into the wind, lift the boom to tilt the sail into the wind. Step under the luffing sail as soon as there is room, then grab the boom and sheet in on the new tack.

PIROUETTE

This is a very pretty trick that involves letting go of the boom while you spin in a 360° circle on the board. Then you grab the boom again before the sail falls and resume sailing.

This is not too difficult if you luff the sail a little and tilt the mast into the wind before you let go. Release the boom quickly and without hesitation, do the pirouette, then grab the boom again. Some sailors have become so good at the pirouette that they can spin through *two* full circles, or 720°, before they grasp the boom again.

WHEELIE

If you have enough wind, this is a spectacular trick on a windsurf board. Get up some speed then move quickly to the rear of the board. Squat down, and at the same time, pull up on the boom. You must be on the centerline with your weight near the stern or you will head up or fall off the wind. If you do everything correctly, the nose of the board will rise up and the board will plow along on its tail with its bow high, just like a drag racer doing a "wheelie."

RIDING-THE-RAIL (RAIL-RIDE)

To do this freestyle trick, get going then step to the downwind side of your board with your back foot. Squat down and bring your front foot down and under the upwind side and help the board up on its side. Now bring your rear foot back up and onto the edge of the board.

The mast is now lying along the top of the board, upright and in a somewhat dangerous position. Too much strain caused by too much leaning or pressure could break the mast or the board in the maststep area. At least the mast might pull out of the maststep and then everything will stop. This is not the easiest trick in the book, but it is exciting to watch. Just sail along standing on the edge of the board.

UPSIDE-DOWN

Some windsurfers can further extend the rail-ride by allowing the board to turn on over, at an angle. It cannot turn all the way over since the mast is still attached to the top (now almost bottom) of the board, but it can be nearly all the way over. The trick is to then stand on the underside of the board, bracing your foot against the daggerboard. Again, not easy at all, but spectacular.

BACK FLIP

Here's a trick that will have them cheering from shore. You kick up between the boom and the sail and do a complete flip around the boom. Be sure you have a good strong boom, a reinforced mast and a good wind before trying this trick. The wind and mast are going to temporarily turn your boom into a backyard gym.

Watch somebody else first, for this trick as well as the others. There are many more not listed here, but you will see dozens of other tricks on the water if you keep watching.

Not that you really need to learn any of them. Windsurfing started out as an enjoyable sport, a healthy and exciting way to

"Riding-the-rail" is a fine trick.

spend some time on the water. Many windsurfers enjoy doing tricks. Many others do not.

RACING

Another enjoyable competitive event for windsurfers is racing. Yacht racing has always been an activity demanding great strategy and skill. Racing on a windsurfer is no different.

Here's a difficult one-footed rail-ride.

There are several excellent books devoted entirely to racing small boats (the differences between them and windsurfers are minimal). Read them for specific discussions on tactics and strategy. There are also a couple of good books now available on windsurfing, with excellent sections on racing. One of them is Ken Winner's and Roger Jones' book, *Windsurfing with Ken Winner.*

Try to imagine this. A long, long line of windsurf boards at the edge of the water. Each has been placed in a position that will be

Here's an "upside-down", with one foot on the daggerboard, but *backwards*, with the daggerboard out of the top of the board. Well, you'll see new tricks every day.

most helpful to its sailor in getting quickly underway. Here the boards are bunched together almost haphazardly. There they are spaced out a little more. On down the beach are two or three boards almost alone. Sails are aiming this way and that.

Now imagine an equally long row of impatient sailors one hundred feet back from the water's edge. They are prancing, dancing, shaking arms and legs and leaning forward. They are waiting with bated breath for a signal to begin running.

At the signal—a horn blast, gunshot or something else not to be missed—the entire horde starts down the beach full speed ahead. They must get to their boards, launch them and get underway as quickly as possible.

Yes, during this "Le Mans Start" of a windsurf race (used most often on long, marathon races), there are runners up and down and end-over-end as they scramble for the boards. It is a comical sight in spite of the seriousness of the occasion.

Then, when the boards are being launched, watch out! It is every sailor for himself or herself. Boards crash into boards, sails tip, one nose will go over another tail, and general pandemonium reigns. Somehow most of the sailors get straightened out and the race is on.

If you want to get into windsurfer racing, study the available books carefully. Windsurfer racing, like all yacht racing, is an intellectual matter. Brains are far more important than brawn, and tactics and strategy are of paramount importance.

CHAPTER

7

Accessories

SELDOM DOES AN ENTERPRISE come along that doesn't immediately create a new business in accessories. Look at the automobile business as a good example.

Windsurfing is no different. You don't even have to buy the basic outfit at one time in one place. You can go here for one segment and there for another. You can buy any one of many different types of boards, sails, masts and other parts.

Skegs and daggerboards come in a variety of sizes and types for different boards and weather conditions.

But suppose you buy a complete outfit from one store, ready to sail. Suppose you go to a local department store, or buy one through the mail, or buy one from the local windsurf shop and carry the whole thing out to your car. There are still many other things you can buy.

Your outfit might have included a wet suit, but if it didn't you will probably want one. Wet suits come in a variety of sizes, colors and types. Is it going to be very cold, or just cold, or cool, or relatively warm? There is a suit for each situation. There is a suit you can wear in the dead of winter, if you love the sport of windsurfing that much. It has a hood, booties, and gloves. Only your face gets cold . . . and it will get cold.

Top. This is a standard "tee" mastfoot. Note the rubber sleeve over the universal joint and the downhaul line.

Bottom. A special mastfoot from Control Products allows the sailor to change the position of the mast.

A harness can be used to support the body and take the strain off the arms. Some of them, like this one, also serve as a backpack.

There is also a simple vest just to hold your body heat on a relatively warm day.

OTHER ACCESSORIES

Here's a partial list of some of the things available for windsurfers. You won't need most of these items, but many of them are fun.

Jewelry, license plate holders, buoyballs for marking a race course, sail mast bags, deluxe sail mast bags, car top racks for carrying your outfit, glue guns and glue sticks for repairing your board, harnesses of all types, including one that carries a six-pack of beverages, windsurfer duffel bags for your personal gear, ring binders for photos and mementos, ice bags, hull decal kits, mast extension for larger sails, safety leashes to fasten the board to the rig, sail streamers to follow wind direction, footstrap kits, display stand to show your outfit when you are not out sailing, books, including this one, magazines (addresses to follow), calendars with beautiful windsurfing pictures, bumper stickers, window decals, posters, films, tee shirts, visors, jerseys, polo shirts, pullover sweaters, jackets, windshirts, windbreakers, sweatshirts, sweatsuits, bikinis, and wristwatches.

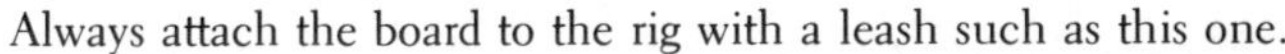

Always attach the board to the rig with a leash such as this one.

And more. And more coming. Windsurfing is here to stay. More than 200,000 windsurf boards were sold worldwide in 1980. The single most popular brand, one of the earliest brands, is *Windsurfer.* It is the world's most popular sailboat. *Windsurfers* are like *Formula Vee* racing cars in automobile racing. They are the single most popular class of all. There are more of them than many of the other classes combined.

There are major windsurfing activity centers in France, Germany, Holland, Japan and several other countries.

A manufacturer-supported association, the International Windsurfer Class Association, was formed in 1973. It helps promote the competitive aspects of the *Windsurfer,* classed as a yacht under IYRU (International Yacht Racing Union) rules. Freestyle and slalom competitions have become very popular among sailors and spectators. Windsurfer Class World Championships have been held

At day's end, some experts tie their sails in the water to keep them clean and easy to handle.

in 1975 in France, in 1976 in the Bahamas, in 1977 in Sardinia, in 1978 in Cancun, Mexico, in 1979 in Clearwater, Florida, in 1980 in the Bahamas, in 1981 in Japan and will be in the Indian Ocean in 1982. They are the largest one-design regattas ever held in the history of yachting. Attendance has broken all previous records each succeeding year.

INSURANCE

You can buy insurance for your outfit, since a recent survey indicates that regular homeowners' insurance might not adequately cover a board and rig. Many associations and clubs provide insurance as a part of membership. To get more information on insurance for your windsurfer, check with your local windsurf equipment store or look in the following publications.

MAGAZINES

The following magazines are interesting, well done and full of color and excitement about the booming sport of windsurfing.

WINDSURF
International Windsurfer Class Association
1955 W. 190th St.
Torrance, CA 90509
(Subscriptions, $15 U.S., $25 foreign)

BOARD AND SAIL
P.O. Box 8108
Sacramento, CA 95818
(Subscriptions, $8 U.S., $10 Canada, $12 foreign)

Once you learn, you'll never forget the thrills of this great sport.

Index